At the Zoo

written by
Carol Kloes

illustrated by
Barbara Dragony

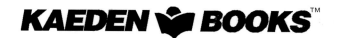

KAEDEN ♥ BOOKS™

We saw bears.

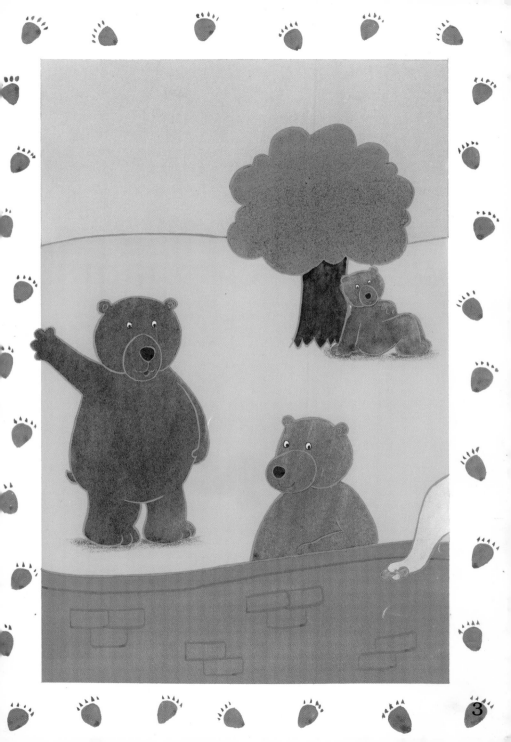

We saw elephants.

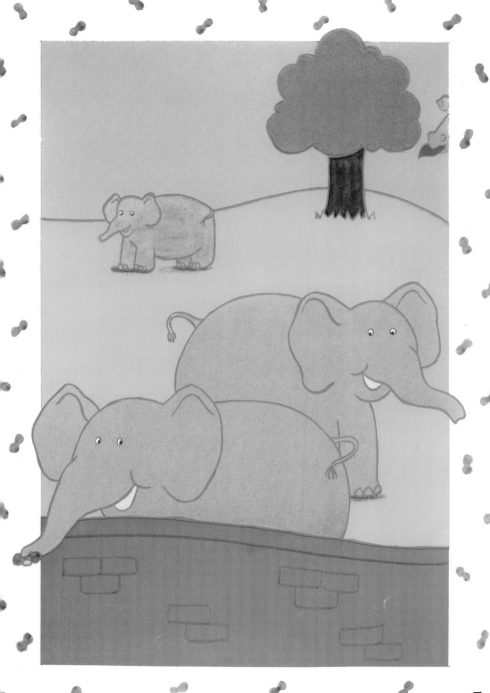

We saw giraffes.

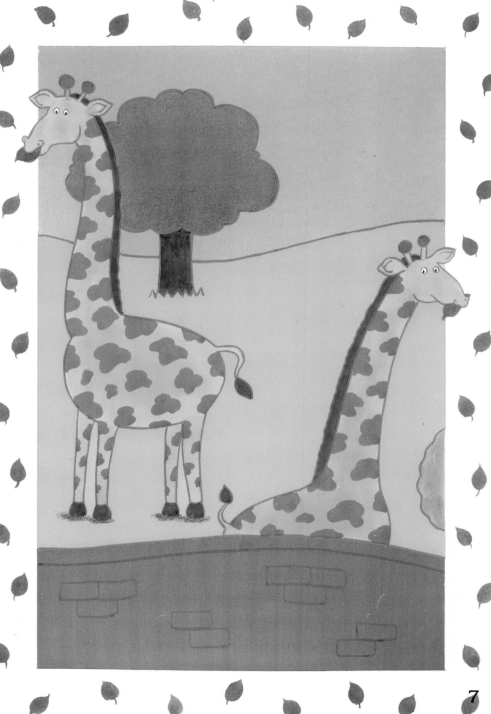

We saw lions.

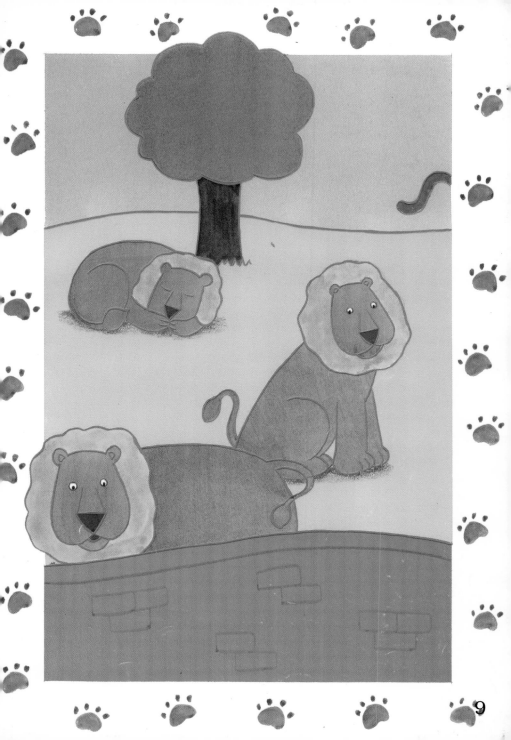

We saw monkeys.

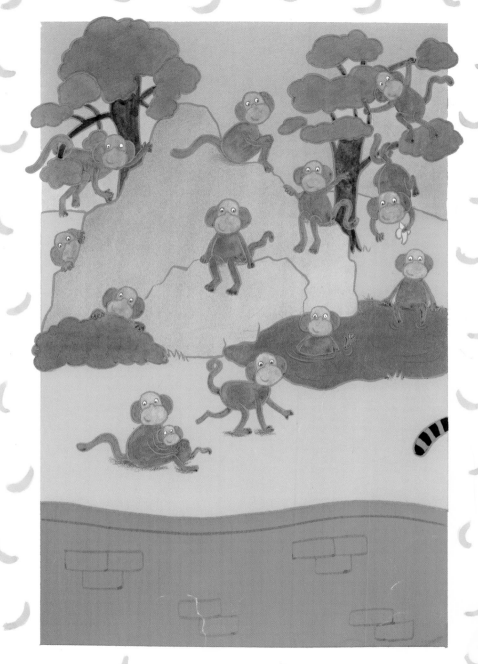

We saw tigers.

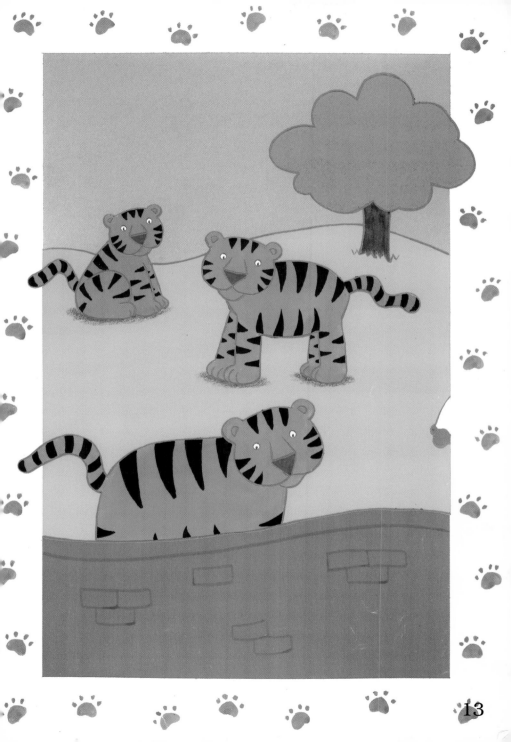

We saw zebras.

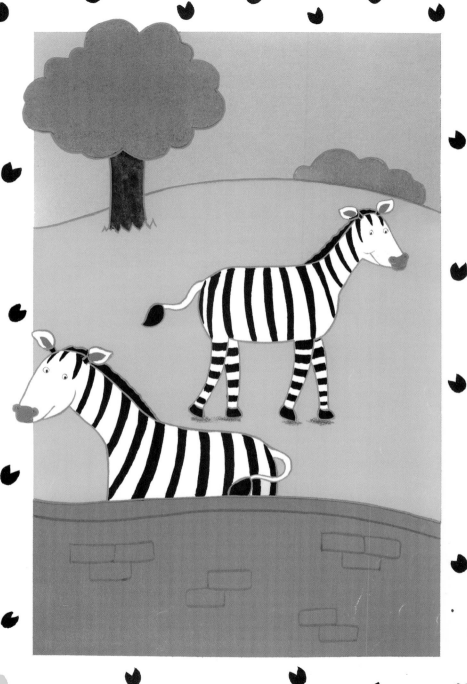

5

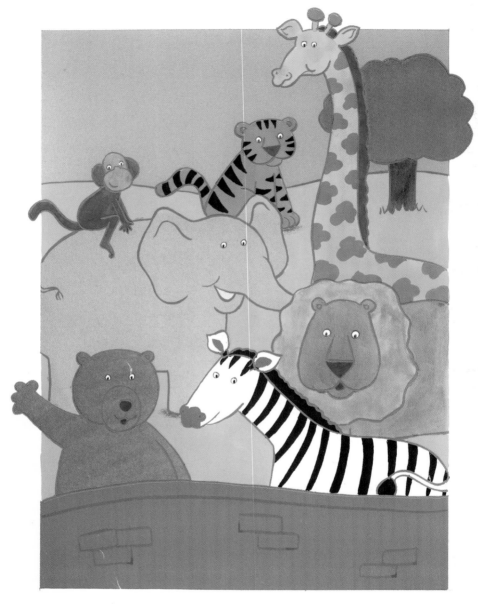

We saw lots of animals at the zoo.